THE MOST
AMAZING
CREATURE
IN THE SEA

BRENDA Z. GUIBERSON

Illustrated by
GENNADY SPIRIN

HENRY HOLT AND COMPANY
NEW YORK

To the amazing Laura Godwin, Julia Sooy, and Patrick Collins
for their creative contributions to this book.
—B. Z. G.

Henry Holt and Company, LLC
Publishers since 1866
175 Fifth Avenue
New York, New York 10010
mackids.com

Henry Holt® is a registered trademark of Henry Holt and Company, LLC.
Text copyright © 2015 by Brenda Z. Guiberson
Illustrations copyright © 2015 by Gennady Spirin

Library of Congress Cataloging-in-Publication Data
Guiberson, Brenda Z., author.
The most amazing creature in the sea / Brenda Z. Guiberson ; illustrated by Gennady Spirin.—First edition.
pages   cm
Audience: Ages 4–8.
ISBN 978-0-8050-9961-4 (hardcover)
1. Marine animals—Juvenile literature. I. Spirin, Gennady, illustrator. II. Title.
QL122.2.G84 2015   591.77—dc23   2014041224

Henry Holt books may be purchased for business or promotional use. For information on
bulk purchases, please contact the Macmillan Corporate and Premium Sales Department at
(800) 221-7945 x5442 or by e-mail at specialmarkets@macmillan.com.

First Edition—2015 / Designed by Patrick Collins
The artist used tempera, watercolor, and pencil on Arches watercolor paper to create the illustrations for this book.
Printed in China by Toppan Leefung Printing Ltd., Dongguan City, Guangdong Province

1 3 5 7 9 10 8 6 4 2

*To all those working to discover and protect
the amazing creatures of the sea*

—B. Z. G.

Who is the most amazing creature in the sea?

I am a **BOX JELLYFISH**.

My venom is the deadliest. I have millions of stinging toxic cells on my tentacles. I kill and digest food quickly so it can't damage my fragile body. I have no brain, no blood, no backbone, and no lungs or gills. But I do have 24 eyes that help me hunt the shrimp and small fish I eat. *That's why I am the most amazing creature in the sea!*

I am a **LEATHERBACK
SEA TURTLE.**

I am the greatest diving reptile on earth. I breathe air, but still I can dive 4,000 feet into the cold, dark ocean and stay underwater for 85 minutes. I love to eat jellyfish. My thick skin shields me from their toxins. Spines in my throat trap their bodies as I swallow them whole. No jellyfish escapes from my gobbling mouth. *That's why I am the most amazing creature in the sea!*

I am a **VAMPIRE SQUID**.

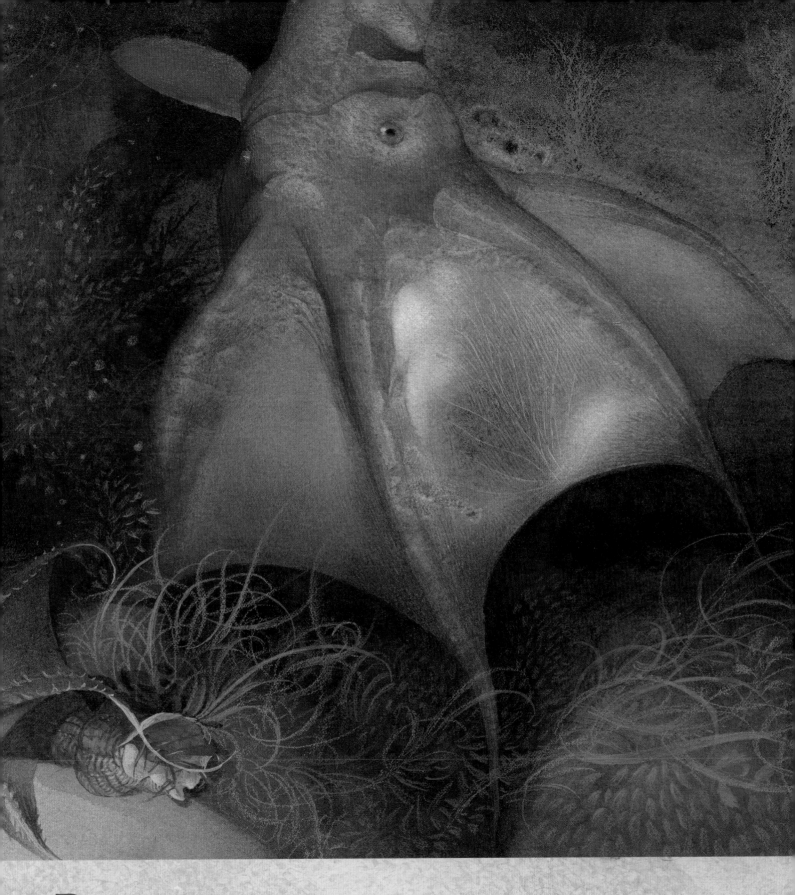

Predators don't stand a chance against my powers of evasion. I can turn inside out to hide in my black cloak. I can also create a dazzling blue light or blue mucus to confuse predators. I have blue blood, and my large gills allow me to live on very little oxygen. I need to feed only every few days, eating old shells and other dead things that drift into the depths. *That's why I am the most amazing creature in the sea!*

I am a **BARRELEYE FISH**.

I wait without moving until my prey swims close. I watch with my amazing green eyes, protected from danger inside my transparent head. I mostly look up, straight through the top of my head, but when I spot my prey, I rotate my eyes to look forward. Then my mouth and eyes are lined up for eating. Watch out, jellyfish! I steal the food you stun with your toxins. *That's why I am the most amazing creature in the sea!*

I am a **MIMIC OCTOPUS.**

A master of disguise, I can take on many appearances. I can swim low across the ocean floor like a flounder. Or I can turn brown and furry and disappear in a clump of algae. I can even masquerade as a toxic lionfish or a sea snake and scare others away. *That's why I am the most amazing creature in the sea!*

I am an ANGLERFISH.

As a female, I lure prey close to my mouth with the light that dangles from my dorsal spine. With my large, toothy jaws, I can swallow animals twice my size. Smaller males join their bodies to mine, latching on with their teeth until their skin fuses into mine. I eat for us all, sharing the nutrients from my bloodstream. I see for us all when each male attached to me loses his eyes. *That's why I am the most amazing creature in the sea!*

I am a **HAGFISH**.

I am also called snot fish for the sticky, slippery slime I secrete when attacked. I have no jaws and no bones. I can tie myself into a knot to squeeze slime off my body. I burrow into dead creatures for a meal and leave the bones for the zombie worms. *That's why I am the most amazing creature in the sea!*

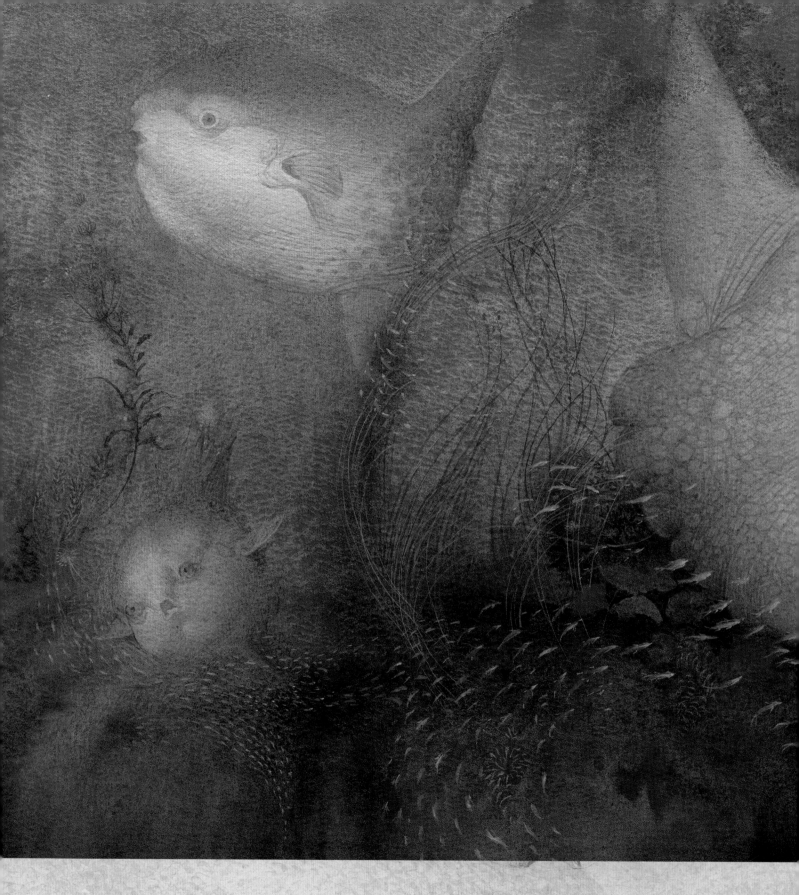

I am an **OCEAN SUNFISH**.

I have up to 300 million eggs in my body—the most of any sea creature! Only a few of these tiny eggs grow up to be big like me. Many parasites collect on my huge body, but cleaner wrasse will nibble them from my skin. I hold the record for heaviest bony fish in the world—I can weigh nearly 5,000 pounds. I am as heavy as a rhinoceros. *That's why I am the most amazing creature in the sea!*

I am a **WHALE SHARK**.

I am the biggest shark, twice as long as the great white shark. My body can grow to be about 40 feet long—that's the length of a school bus. Though I am so large, I quickly slurp up the smallest of sea creatures, filtering plankton and small fish like menhaden from the water with my wide mouth. I am an eating machine. *That's why I am the most amazing creature in the sea!*

I am a **BLUE WHALE**.

Everything about me is supersized. My tongue is as heavy as an elephant. My heart is the size of a car. My baby weighs 6,000 pounds at birth. Every day he drinks 100 gallons of fatty milk, gaining more than eight pounds in an hour. We both need lots of energy. My throat expands to take in 17,000 gallons of food-filled water in a single mouthful, eating about 40 million krill every day. I am the most colossal creature to ever live on earth. *That's why I am the most amazing creature in the sea!*

I am a LEAFY SEA DRAGON.

Just try to find me! I have no teeth or stomach and am a very slow swimmer, so I stay hidden to feed constantly. My appendages wave in the water like seaweed; they are my camouflage—among the best and most elaborate of all animals. All my beautiful parts help me drift and tumble with the current. I can even change color. *That's why I am the most amazing creature in the sea!*

I am a **WOLFFISH**.

My natural antifreeze keeps my blood flowing in the icy water I call home. I have fangs and crushing teeth. There are even teeth in my throat to help me crunch through the hard shells of oysters, sea urchins, lobsters, and crabs. My teeth wear down quickly, so every year I grow a new set. *That's why I am the most amazing creature in the sea!*

We are **HELPERS**.

Without us, the other creatures of the sea could not survive. We are menhaden and oysters; we filter water and keep it clean so plants can grow. We are sea urchins that gobble algae so coral can grow. We are coral that hide small fish and shrimp. We are remora and wrasse that clean big fish. We are millions of billions of krill that feed the whale. *That's why we are the most amazing creatures in the sea!*

So which sea creature is the most amazing?

Is it the one with the most deadly venom, the blue blood, or the rotating eyes?
Or is it the master of disguise, the one with the most eggs, the best light,
or the most slime?

Or is it the biggest shark, the most colossal creature, the one with the best camouflage, the best antifreeze, or all the helpers who make it possible for the others to survive? Or could it be another sea creature, maybe one not yet discovered?

You decide.

Author's Note

A vast amount of all life on earth is in the oceans. Studying it can be like a trip into outer space. Scientists need special ships. They bring oxygen. They search in cold places, bubbly places, and dark places where the force of deep water presses in on all sides. So far they have found and identified about 250,000 different marine species, but they are just beginning. Would you like to become an ocean scientist? Millions of mysterious sea creatures are yet to be discovered. They will be amazing, using incredible defenses like camouflage, lights, speed, size, venom, slime, and mimicry to allow them to live in places where people can go only if they have special equipment.

Sea creatures have been around for millions of years, yet today many find it hard to survive. Leatherback sea turtles die after eating drifting plastic that looks like jellyfish or getting caught in a fishing net. Wolffish get scooped up in fishing gear that scrapes the ocean floor. Great schools of menhaden have been fished from the seas, reducing their numbers by an alarming amount.

If leatherbacks and other jellyfish predators aren't around, then jellyfish populations explode, clogging ship valves and closing beaches. When wolffish aren't present, sea urchins increase and gobble up too much kelp. When menhaden are fished out, the unfiltered water gets murky, sea plants don't get enough sunlight, and creatures can't find their food. Declining populations of menhaden also mean less food for tuna, toothed whales, dolphins, bluefish, mackerel, cod, swordfish, crabs, lobsters, osprey, pelicans, gannets, gulls, and others that rely on this oily protein.

Today less than 1 percent of the oceans are places where sea creatures can thrive without interference from humans. Several groups, like the Menhaden Defenders and the Ocean Conservancy, are working hard to change this. Find out how more organizations like these are helping to preserve the most amazing creatures in the sea—and look for ways that you can help too!

Bibliography

Cole, Brandon, and Michael Scott. *Reef Life: A Guide to Tropical Marine Life.* Buffalo, NY: Firefly Books, 2013.

Crist, Darlene Trew, Gail Scowcroft, and James M. Harding, jr. *World Ocean Census: A Global Survey of Marine Life.* Buffalo, NY: Firefly Books, 2009.

Franklin, H. Bruce. *The Most Important Fish in the Sea: Menhaden and America.* Washington, DC: Shearwater, 2008.

Jenkins, Steve. *Down, Down, Down: A Journey to the Bottom of the Sea.* Boston: HMH Books for Young Readers, 2009.

Knowlton, Nancy. *Citizens of the Sea: Wondrous Creatures From the Census of Marine Life.* Washington, DC: National Geographic, 2010.

Nouvian, Claire. *The Deep: The Extraordinary Creatures of the Abyss.* Chicago: University of Chicago Press, 2007.

Online

animals.nationalgeographic.com/animals/sharks/

aquariumofpacific.org

bbc.co.uk/nature/habitats/Deep_sea

marinebio.org

menhadendefenders.org

ocean.nationalgeographic.com/ocean/

oceanconservancy.org/healthy-ocean/